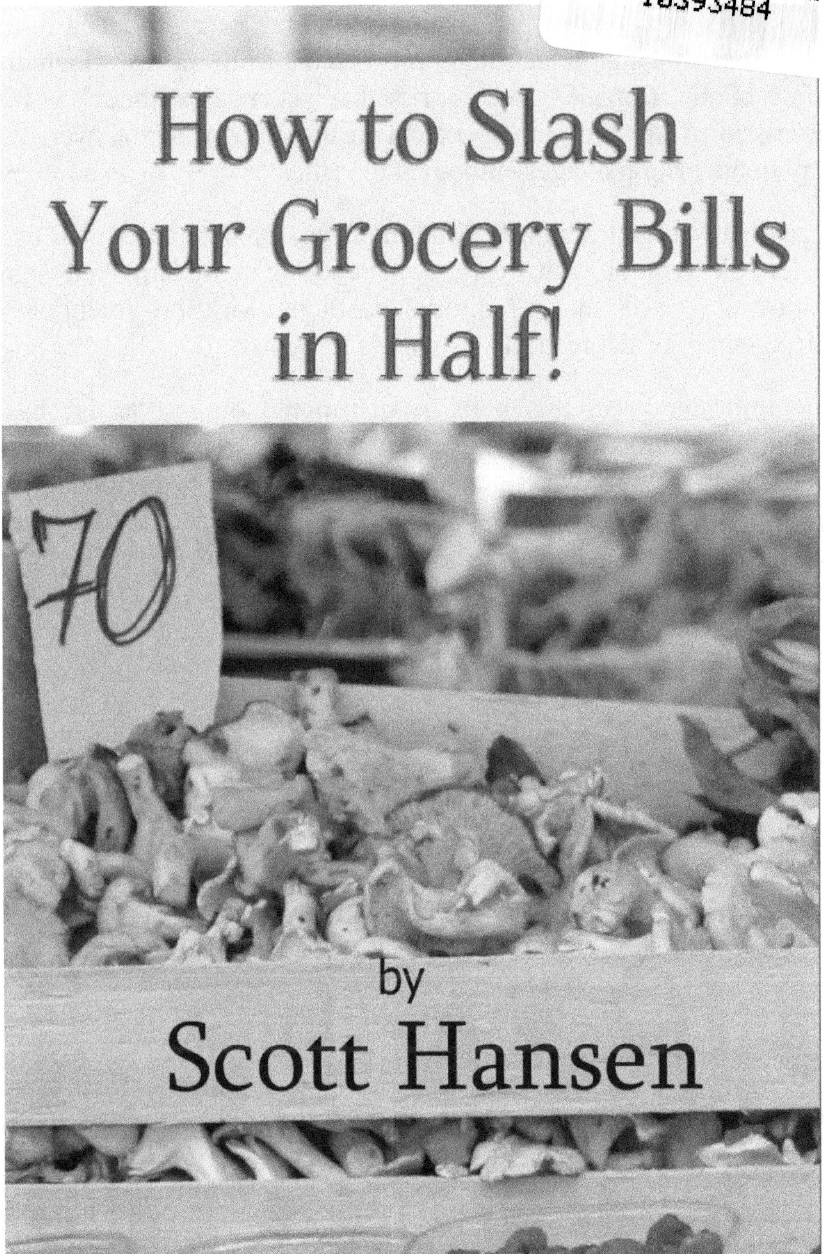

How to Slash Your Grocery Bills in Half!

by

Scott Hansen

Please check out my other books on www.amazon.com.

Scott Hansen

scotthanse@gmail.com

TABLE OF CONTENTS

Preface

1. Equipment Needed for Storing Food

   Buying a Freezer

   A Food Vacuum System

   The Gripstic™

   Plastic Containers

2. Storing Your Food

   Setting up a Pantry

   Long-Term Food Storage

   Canned Foods

   Other Food Necessities

   Freeze-Dried and Dehydrated Foods

   The Best Foods for Long-Term Storage

   Frozen Food Storage

3. Grocery Shopping Ins and Outs

   Always Changing Grocery Prices

   Easy Ways to Slash Your Grocery Bill

   Planning your Meals in Advance

   The Grocery Game

   How to Plan Extended Menus

   Couponing for the Common Man

   Tracking Your Waste

4. Grocery Store Tricks and Tips

Do not Buy Items from your Grocery Store that you can Buy Elsewhere.

The Grocery Store Layout

How to shop: Different Grocery Stores, Different Prices

Things to Keep in Mind:

Is Convenience Worth the Price?

5. Other Grocery Store Tips

Saving Beyond the Grocery Store

Preface

Look around you and you know that food prices are rising higher than the cost of living and rising higher than your wages. This winter as I write this book the price of bacon is supposed to double. This past summer the price of butter fluctuated wildly, almost doubling in price at one point. Getting a handle on your food bill each month will put money in your pocket and you will end up eating healthier as well.

The government says food prices will rise between 4-6% the year this book was written. Over the course of my lifetime this number was fairly consistent when averaged out over the years. The government predicts that a family of four will spend about $12,300 a year on food. If you could cut this number in half you would save $6,150 a year. If you do this year in and year out you will put a lot of money in your family's pocket.

You have to eat. There is no way to survive unless you eat. When you eat out at a fast food place or a restaurant, your food bill is more than if you ate at home because you pay for the convenience and you pay for the ambiance. When you come home from a long day at work there is nothing easier than telling your family that you are going to eat out that night. But with the economy getting tighter more families are now eating at home. Your cost of groceries will rise the less you eat out, but you still will be saving a lot of money in the long run.

When you grocery shop I want you to think outside the box and not always go to your local grocery store. Groceries can be bought anywhere from a Super Target to a cut-rate priced store like Aldi. You may have to drive a bit more and spend a little more time shopping, but the tradeoff is worth it and you will save money.

A lot of foods you buy in your grocery store are over-packaged and over-priced. You will see big packaging compensate for the product inside that is mostly air. Companies spend billions of dollars to make packaging look attractive. They design and test this packaging to have the most visual impact and to get you to part with your money. If you figure this out and shop wisely, you will notice there are a ton of different options even within the same product categories.

I have successfully implemented the methods used in this book to cut my family's food bills. The changes are painless and easy. When you take the steps listed in this book you will find you are suddenly flush with money, more money than you had before. You will also start to enjoy planning and cooking meals for you family and the appeal of going out to dinner will begin to fade.

Read this book. It is divided into different sections and each section deals with a different aspect of shopping for food and saving money. Each section is laid out in a logical fashion which will make it easy to read, easy to understand, and most importantly easy to implement.

1. Equipment Needed for Storing Food

The biggest aspect of setting up a food purchasing program is to think about food storage. No matter how much money you spend on food you have to have a place to store it when you get home. If food is not stored correctly then you will end up throwing food products away which is the same as flushing your money down the toilet. Some things mentioned are common sense, and other things mentioned might be new to you. I learn new things every day so I have learned to be flexible when it comes to food and food storage.

There are some upfront costs with food storage. You will have to come up with money out of pocket to purchase these items if you want to save on food costs in the long term. If you cannot afford these items, my tips for cutting costs at the grocery store will still help you save money, just not as much money as you could. I have researched the prices on these expensive items as of this writing, and I will offer some options on where to purchase these items at a cheaper price.

Buying a Freezer

The first item you will need to purchase will be a freezer. A stand-alone freezer will allow you to purchase food in bulk and more importantly will allow you to keep the food in pristine condition for up to a year. There are two types of freezers, chest freezers which start out at about $180 at Sears if purchased new, and standup freezers which start at about $260 new at Sears. Each has advantages and disadvantages.

Chest freezers hold more food per cubic foot than standup freezers. There are no shelves and everything just gets stacked on top of each other. They are square in shape and are accessed through a door on top. The major disadvantage is that you will have to dig for food to find it. Food gets buried and is sometimes lost at the bottom of the chest.

Standup freezers take up less of a footprint, but they give up storage space for shelves. You will not be able to fit as much food in a standup freezer compared to a chest freezer. It is easy to find food in these types of freezers because when you open the door all your food is neatly stacked on shelves. You can easily eyeball the contents of your freezer. I prefer this type of freezer but it is all up to personal choice.

A chest freezer uses less energy than a standup model. A chest freezer runs more efficiently than a standup model. Finally, a full freezer is more efficient than a half-full freezer with either model.

The great thing about buying appliances is that they go on sale all the time. You can look at weekly ads and see these items on sale all the time. You can also buy freezers at stores like Costco and Sam's Club. They do not have the variety there, but you do get a lot of bang for your buck when you buy one there.

Another option is to buy a freezer at an outlet store. There are a few outlet stores in the city I live in and most of these stores have sales on top of their already low prices. You can find overstock freezers here as well as freezers that have scratches and dents, or freezers that have been returned. If you are willing to give up cosmetic beauty for function, you can walk away with a great running freezer for a relatively low price.

Ask friends and family or post something on Facebook letting your friends and acquaintances know you are looking to purchase a stand-alone freezer and ask for suggestions on where to go, or see if anyone has a freezer they are no longer using. You might get lucky and find one for free or very cheap.

Finally, I love Craigslist. I purchase things from Craigslist all the time and I never have had a bad experience. If you go to Craigslist and click on your city, simply type "freezer" in the search box and you will get listings for a lot of different freezers. You will also get listings for anything that has a freezer being sold with it; for instance refrigerator freezers. Be diligent and look every day, and multiple times a day. If you look hard you will find someone selling a great freezer at a very low price.

Finally, where should you keep your freezer? Do not run your freezer in the garage. In the summer the garage gets too hot and the freezer will have to run extra hard to keep cool. Today's refrigerators and freezers are not designed to run in very warm or very cold temperatures, thus a garage is a bad option.

A basement is ideal to keep a freezer. It is out of sight and out of mind. If you and in a condo or apartment building a freezers could be kept in a maintenance room. If neither is available it can usually be placed anywhere and you do not need to buy a gigantic freezer for this to work.

A Food Vacuum System

A food vacuum packaging device helps get air out of bags where food is stored. Air is the enemy of food storage because air causes freezer burn in food stored in your freezer, and air is the catalyst for mold in your refrigerator or closet shelf. When you buy a machine you will also need to buy specially designed bags that help get the air out. The bags can get a little pricey, but you can wash them and reuse them until you run out of room to seal them.

There are a few different makers of this product with the most popular one being the FoodSaver™ brand. You can find a basic model for around $100 online. I found several models for sale on Craigslist in my area that are brand new and in the box, for half of that or $50. I know that all kinds of stores sell these products including Sears, Target, Costco and Kohls. If you wait until there is a sale you can get a brand new model at a fairly reasonable price.

Like razors, though, these companies make money on the bags and not the vacuum unit. The bags can get quite costly in comparison with the sealing unit itself. I have found that shopping for these bags online makes the bags much cheaper. You can also purchase these bags at your local warehouse club to help bring down your costs. The bags are cut and sealed, and can be re-used over and over again as long as you have enough room to seal the bag.

The Gripstic™

Have you ever used chip clips to try to keep chips fresh and make them last longer? They are not very effective, are they? You put them on a bag of chips and the chips go stale at about exactly the same rate as if you had used nothing at all.

I came across a product called the Gripstic™. I do not own any stock in this company or have any vested interest in it. I came across their products at the Minnesota State Fair in a vendor's booth in the Grandstand. My mom had turned me onto them. This product is amazing. They are little plastic devices that you use to keep chip bags closed, cheese bags closed, really any product closed that comes in a bag. When you use one of these clips you push the air out of the bag and then use a Gripstic™ to close it. All the air stays out and your food will last a lot, lot longer. I have found that my chips last about four times as long using a grip stick instead of a bag clip. They are relatively inexpensive, and when you buy a set you will wish that you had bought more. They really are a miracle product.

A package of 14 of these in various sizes is about $20.

Here is there web site: http://www.gripstic.com/.

Plastic Containers

A good food storage system also uses plastic containers to store long lasting perishables. The plastic containers keep out the air and moisture and will allow longer lasting foods to stay dry and fresh for a longer period of time. Plastic containers are susceptible to rodent infestations, but if you store your food where there will be rodents just be sure to set plenty of traps outside of the food storage bins.

You can use big plastic containers to store things like wheat and grains, rice, beans and other long-lasting food items. Make sure the plastic bins you buy are safe for food storage.

2. Storing Your Food

Storing food takes preparation and planning. Besides purchasing a freezer and a food vacuum system, you will need to create a pantry space where you can store canned goods and regular store purchases. You will need to implement some basic principles used in storing food; that is you will need to keep an eye on the expiration dates of items you buy and you will need to rotate your stock of items in your freezer or pantry.

It is sometimes helpful, but more work, to keep an itemized list for items in your freezer, your pantry and the bulk dry goods that you have stored elsewhere. Having an itemized list in a spreadsheet, where you have a column listing the food item, a column with the purchase date and a column with the expiration date, will allow you to sort the items you have by any one of the three categories.

Here is a link to a free program that will keep track of food items in your house: http://www.download32.com/staples-for-handbase-i66147.html.

Here is a link that rates the best apps for iPhones and android apps: http://appadvice.com/appguides/show/grocery-list-helpers.

Setting up a Pantry

Your home may already have a nice sized pantry. If this is the case then you are good to go on cutting your food bill in half.

If your house does not have a pantry you will need a cool, dry place to store your canned and dry goods. If you have an extra closet you can purchase affordable shelves from your local home improvement store and create an expanded pantry space. Avoid bathroom closets because the humidity and heat from the shower make it a poor choice and your food will spoil faster.

Get creative. If you have a closet that is in use, move the items from that closed to under your bed storage containers, or store these items elsewhere. This will allow you to use your existing closet as a food pantry.

Long-Term Food Storage

The cheapest foods to buy almost always have the longest shelf life. When you buy this type of food in bulk you will be saving money, and you will be hedging your bets against rising food prices in the future. Buying 25 pounds of rice is cheaper than buying a box of Uncle Ben's rice. Grains and beans are cheaper when you buy in bulk as well.

While purchasing this type of food is economical, it is important to note that it still needs to be rotated, it still needs to be stored properly, and even though some items will last for hundreds of years, you will still need to protect these items from air, water, rot, and rodents.

The following sections will deal with the shelf lives of the most common type of foods people buy. It is important to know this information so you do not go out and buy items that you cannot possibly consume by the time the product expires on the shelf.

Canned Foods

Buy any canned food at the store and you will see an expiration date on that food. Most have a relatively short shelf life. The most you will get out of canned food is about a year for most foods, with the nutritional value of these foods tapering off after about six months of being in a can. Most likely you can eat the food that is a year old but you will not be getting all the nutrition out of the food and it most likely will not taste very good.

There are some exceptions to this rule. For instance, canned meats tend to have more preservatives in them and they can last well over a year and not lose taste or nutrition. Salted and cured meats and fish can last for up to three years.

Honey is not technically a canned food but honey will last forever if it is stored properly. Honey has been found in Egyptian tombs and was still edible. If you store honey in a cool dry place out of the sunlight, it can last forever at room temperature. It can crystalize, but if this happens (i.e. it looks cloudy) just put the jar in a pan and heat the pan slowly until the crystals dissolve.

If the outside window for canned food is an 18 month shelf life, then this will limit how much food you can store. You must eat the older canned food if you do not want it to go to waste. Make sure that when you cook your meal that you use the oldest cans first. If you do not, you will just be throwing the food away in the end and that is a big waste of money.

So how much canned food should you keep on hand? If you can build up your supply to cover nine months of meals, then you will have enough food to ride out most emergencies. This means you need to keep a list of food items you will use for your meals and you must do a little planning on what your future meals will look like.

If you do not want to put that much thought into it you can always purchase dehydrated food, which is covered in a later section. Dehydrated food costs more than "normal" food because of the amount of development it takes to create this food. It is designed to have a shelf life of up to 25 years, and although it is not cheap it is certainly a viable alternative to having food on hand for major emergencies.

So when you shop, put the newest cans of food in the back of your pantry. Take out the older cans and move them to the front of your pantry; doing this will make you naturally take out the oldest cans first.

Other Food Necessities

Pasta products can last in your pantry for up to two years. Pasta is easy to store and easy to prepare, and it goes on sale frequently. Since it lasts up to two years you can store more of it and always have plenty on hand for your everyday needs.

Flour has a shelf life of about one year, but you can also freeze flour and it will last up to two years. Flour is so flexible and you can make so many different meals from it, and all you need are spices and minimal other ingredients to make a meal. It is important to store flour in a cool dry place for maximum shelf life.

Vegetable oils tend to have a shelf life of about one year if they are unopened and then when you open them you usually have a six month window to use them. Olive oil will last a little longer, up to a year when opened or a couple of years if unopened. The best type of oil to have on hand for food storage or emergencies is a solid shortening like Crisco. If left unopened and stored in a cool dry place, a product like Crisco (which does have preservatives) will last 8-10 years.

It is very important for all the above mentioned food items that you rotate your stock or use it before the expiration date or else you will end up throwing your groceries out.

Freeze-Dried and Dehydrated Foods

If you are looking for food that will keep a long time and is ideal for food emergency situations then freeze dried or dehydrated foods are a great option. Some dehydrated foods have a shelf live, if unopened, of more than 25 years. When you open the can, though, it must be used within a week or two before it goes bad.

The up side is that freeze dried or dehydrated foods tend to taste better than canned foods and these foods are easy to prepare, you just add water and warm them up. In an emergency situation you would need a good quality water storage option as well.

I will not go into this section more than I already have because dehydrated or freeze dried food falls into the realm of emergency food storage and it gets away from cutting your food bill in half. If you want more information on these types of food there are plenty of web sites on the internet that will help you make good choices for these foods.

Costco has a section on their website dedicated to long-term food storage. If you simply want to buy food for food emergencies, I would check their website out. You can buy enough freeze-dried food to feed a family of four for a year for about $4,000.00. These items have a 25 year shelf life. Please see this link for details: http://www.costco.com/all-emergency-food.html

The Best Foods for Long-Term Storage

Long term food storage consists of food that will last for years. The best long-term food storage items are grains and rice, coffees and teas, cocoa, salt, sugar, and spices. Over time these foods may lose some of their taste but they will remain edible. If you keep them cool and dry, they'll last a very, very long time.

Let's start with the smallest items first. Spices will last a very long time if stored properly. Spices will not go bad; rather they will lose their potency and flavor over time. Most spices will last two years with no problems. If you freeze spices they will last much, much longer, perhaps up to four or five years.

Salt gets a paragraph all its own. Salt is used in canning, it is used to cure meats, it is used for flavor in many dishes, and it is a basic food item that every pantry should have. If there is ever a food emergency, salt could be used to barter for other items. Salt will last forever without losing its taste or effectiveness.

Sugar has an indefinite shelf life as well. It will get hard over time, but it is still edible and you can still use it when you cook.

Rice will last for up to 30 years in storage. For long-term food storage it is recommended that you have about 50 lbs. of rice per person, per year and a total of 300 lbs. of a combination of rice and grains. Rice should be stored in airtight containers and you should purchase food-safe oxygen absorbers to put in the rice.

Other grains, such as whole wheat, should be stored the same as rice. Whole wheat can last up to 30 years if stored properly. Dent corn is the whole grain form of corn and you can make corn meal out of it. If you store it in its most natural form, dent corn, it too can last up to 30 years. The same goes for groats, which are the whole grain form of oats. Store all of these items in food-safe, air-tight containers with food moisture absorbers stored with them and they will last you a lifetime.

Unprocessed grains give you the most bang for the buck and when they are stored properly, they last a very long time. This makes whole unprocessed grains ideal for many people who have the space to store them. It would be possible to store enough rice and grains for a family of four for a year for under $1,000 dollars and these items can be stored for up to 30 years.

If you're going to store grains like these for processing, then you should also store packets of dry yeast. Packets of dry yeast can last on your shelf for up to two years and they may last longer in your freezer. Yeast and grains will allow you to bake your own bread in case of a food emergency.

Dried beans, soybeans, oats, barley, corn, and other grains will all last up to 30 years if you take care to keep them cool and dry. Once your food and grains are purchased and stored away in a basement in the airtight plastic containers they come in, they can be forgotten about until they are needed.

The main thing to be aware of when storing grains and beans is rodent infestation. If your basement has rodents, be sure to set traps out around the food to kill the vermin before they get into your food storage.

Frozen Food Storage

When you purchase a freezer and start using it to store your food, it is very important that you go through it periodically to ensure that you use the older items first and that the newer items are put in the back or at the bottom of the freezer. It is infuriating to have to throw away old frozen food.

Freezer burn is the most common reason you will need to throw out food from your freezer. The good news is that you can absolutely limit the amount of damage that freezer burn can do to your food. Freezer burn gives food a dry leathery look. Foods with freezer burn may be safe to eat, but the general look and feel of these items make them almost unpalatable.

The following will help you maintain a well-stocked and clean freezer:

1. Keep your frozen food well organized. This means that you should write the date on the packages when you purchase them before they go into the freezer. It is advisable to keep a list of everything in your freezer. Add to this list when new items go in and take items off the list when you use them. It takes a while to get used to doing this but when you do you will have a reliable food supply.

2. Most items sold as frozen food comes in flimsy packaging that cannot withstand long-term storage in a freezer. Think of frozen vegetables. When you have flimsy packaging it is best to repackage these items using a vacuum sealing product or using freezer bags.

3. Air is the enemy in a freezer. Remove as much air as possible from the freezer bag or container before you store it, or better yet have a vacuum sealer do the work for you.

4. Use your refrigerator freezer for short-term storage only. Anything you are going to store long-term should go into a

chest or upright freezer. Items in your long-term storage freezer will still need to be rotated but not as often as your refrigerator freezer.

Remember, the more food you have in your freezer the more efficiently it runs.

3. Grocery Shopping Ins and Outs

Always Changing Grocery Prices

Grocery prices always rise for a variety of reasons. Sometimes it is because food is in or out of season; you will pay more for strawberries in the winter than in the summer. Sometimes it is because we use corn to create ethanol to add to our gasoline. As the scarcity of corn rises, so do the prices. Chicken and cattle are fed a corn diet and if it costs more to feed the animals then the price of your chicken or steak will rise as well. When gasoline prices rise it raises the cost of everything in the grocery store because it takes gas to get the products to the stores, to get them from the manufacturers, to produce things on the farm. So if the price of gas goes up it has a domino effect on the things you buy in the store every week. Finally, inflation alone adds to the cost of groceries at the store.

Second, we live in a global economy. The corn our farmers grow can be sold to world markets and they will sell to the people that give them the best price. As more and more countries become prosperous the demand for food rises, and the prices go up everywhere.

Finally, whenever there is drought or too much rain, this effects the crop production and this in turn drives up food prices. This means that food prices will continue to climb even though the demand in the U.S. is pretty much stable. The tough part is that food prices are rising higher than the rate of inflation.

So grocery prices will continue to rise. What can you do to control this? This chapter deals with things you can do outside of the grocery store in order to control your costs. This involves keeping track of the things you purchase every week, and this involves some long-term planning on your part.

Easy Ways to Slash Your Grocery Bill

The easiest way to cut the costs of your grocery bill is to examine your current shopping habits. This means you will have to do some basic menu planning, you will have to start cutting coupons, and you will have to start considering buying things in bulk. If you implement this strategy then you will absolutely cut your grocery bill down to size.

For instance, let' say your family eats ten pounds of ground beef in a month. If you pay $4.00 a pound normally you would be spending $40.00 a month on ground beef alone. If you shop at Costco or Sam's Club you can get a large package of ground beef for $2.50 a pound. This would save you $15.00 each and every month on just ground beef. Beef is one of the items that frequently go on sale so you can find reduced prices at many different places. As long as you are prepared and have a freezer, you will be saving a lot of money.

Think of your purchases in cost per unit. In the ground beef example above the cost per unit is the price per pound. For other items it will most likely be cost per ounce, or in the case of soda, cost per can. Just because something is available at Sam's Club or Costco, does not necessarily mean that the price per unit is cheaper. You will have to start paying attention to the cost per unit and you will have to have a calculator with you when you go shopping.

Planning your Meals in Advance

A lot of people plan their menus out the morning of the meal or maybe a day in advance. This means your family decides on a meal and then you go buy the main ingredients you need to make the meal. No thought is given to cost or price and no thought is made to purchase items for future use.

You can easily plan for a weeks' worth of meals, or even a months' worth of meals and then significantly cut down on the cost of each meal. If you know you will be needing 10 pounds of ground beef in a month you can go to Sam's Club or Costco and buy that item in bulk and you will save a lot of money. If you will be eating the same side dishes more than once a month, then you can plan to buy in bulk or find the item on sale.

With places like Sam's Club or Costco you do not always have to wait for sales to get the best prices on meat. The prices on meat at both these places are usually better than what my grocery store offers and the meat seems to be higher quality. Your grocery store will occasionally be able to beat these prices, so it is a good idea to know what items cost where you live. If you see a deal that is too good to pass up then you should jump all over it.

The Grocery Game

The Grocery Game is a website (www.thegrocerygame.com) that promises you will save on average, 67% off of your current grocery bill. I have read reviews and most people claimed to have saved around 50% off their grocery bill. The way the web site works is you enter your zip code and a list of stores that are in their database appears. You check off the stores you want to use (it cost $10 every 8 weeks for the first store, and $5 more for each additional store you add) and the Grocery Game will find all the items that are on sale for the upcoming week. The site matches the sales with available coupons. This means that you will have to buy the Sunday paper (or a couple of Sunday papers) in order to take full advantage of The Grocery Game.

The Grocery Game is divided into several color-coded sections based on how much you will save. For instance, items in black are good deals but you should buy them only if you need them. Blue items are what they call investing items, I would call them items you keep in food storage. They are half off and a great buy. Green items are the free items. Yes, it is possible to get items for free from the grocery store.

If you want to simplify your life and you do not mind paying a little money every two months, then I would recommend The Grocery Game. The first month is free but the following months cost money. From everything I have read, the service is absolutely worth the subscription price.

How to Plan Extended Menus

This is the toughest part of saving money on groceries for most families simply because it is not something most of us do each and every day. It takes time and commitment to plan out what you are going to eat for the next two weeks or the next month. Breakfast and lunch are usually the easiest because most people eat the same thing every day for breakfast and they eat a variation of the same thing for lunch. Dinner is where it gets complex.

If you plan out your menu for two weeks or a month in advance (I always break it down into two week chunks) you can figure out what main ingredients you will need to execute those menus. For example if you planned out a two week menu that had hamburgers, chicken enchiladas, pork chops, a pot roast, and fish, each week then you would have different ingredients for each night of the week, and you could use each ingredient once each week.   This gets to be a bit more complex.

You could tweak this menu a bit to have a meat and chicken themed menu one week and a hamburger and seafood menu the second week. This means you would be buying less of the main items for your ingredients (because you can split them up and use different parts of the chicken for different meals) and thus you would cut down on waste.

For the side items you can buy canned or frozen vegetables and use them as needed. If you have a salad with every meal the ingredients for that will not change much and you will have all the items on hand at all times. By careful planning you can cut down on waste and you can save money on your overall bill.

Couponing for the Common Man

Extreme couponing is the latest rage right now because of all the reality TV shows that feature people that do this. They will buy four or five grocery carts full of items and go to the grocery store on double coupon days and end up paying a very low price for hundreds, or even a thousand dollars' worth of groceries. These people go for the deal just to get the deal. There is no way they can use all the products they buy so they end up giving a lot of these items to charity and food shelves. They also supply their families with all the dish and laundry detergent that they could ever use.

That being said, coupons can really save you money. You have to be careful because you do not want to use coupons on items you do not or would not use; this would be wasting food and money. If you go the coupon route it might be worth your while to sign up for The Grocery Game mentioned in a previous section. This web site will tell you exactly what coupons to use and in what stores to use them.

Stores reported that last year shoppers redeemed almost $5 billion dollars' worth of coupons. Shoppers themselves report an average of 12 percent savings on their grocery bills from coupons. If you use The Grocery Game site they claim you can save up to 67% on your grocery bill.

Tips for coupons:

1. Get the Sunday paper, or a couple of Sunday papers, and collect coupons for items you normally buy.
2. Check out the grocery store ads in the Sunday papers because these ads usually have in-store coupons inside of their ads as well as sale prices for that week that need no coupons.
3. Go to web sites online that specialize in grocery coupons. http://www.couponmom.com is a free website where you can

find grocery coupons or coupons that are specific to the store you shop at. http://www.grocerycouponnetwork.com/ is a web site that simply has coupons you would use on everyday items.

4. If you have local stores that have double coupon days then shop on those days only. These stores will double the amount of any coupon you bring into their store, usually up to a certain limit.

5. Ask if your grocery store will match other competitor's coupons. Target and Wal-Mart will always do this if you bring in a competitors ad.

6. Sign up for your stores membership cards. These cards offer extra deals for you, sometimes it is cheaper gas, and sometimes you save money off your total bill. Make sure you read the fine print and are OK with their policies.

7. Get a coupon wallet. This is used to hold all your coupons and you can separate them by product type or grocery aisle. They are easy to carry and it will make lie a lot less stressful than carrying around a handful of store coupons.

Tracking Your Waste

This may be the dumbest advice I give in this book. If you buy less food you will spend less money. You can buy less food if you do not buy the food you usually throw away. It is estimated by our government that each person in the United States throws away about 225 pounds of food per year. For a family of four this means about 1,000 pounds. It suddenly sounds like a lot of food when you talk about it this way.

Here is how to keep track of wasted food:

1. Buy a notebook and keep it in your kitchen.
2. Every time you clean your freezer and refrigerator, every time you clean out your pantry or cupboard, or every time

you throw away things on your plate after a meal, keep track of that food in the notebook

3. Do this for at least two weeks and at best a month. You will see patterns that start to emerge. Maybe those Brussel sprouts are not going over as well as you thought and you are simply buying them, cooking them, and then putting them in a landfill. Cut out the middle man and save money.

4. If you consistently throw out rotten potatoes or onions, cut back and quit buying the big bags of those items. While you might pay more per unit for these items, in the long run you will save money if you are not throwing them out each week. If those items are going bad because of the way you store them it might be worth it to research the best practices to storing these items. Maybe you are simply storing things wrong.

These small steps will save you a few bucks every week, but those few bucks can add up to hundreds of dollars over the course of a year. You do not have to eat poorly, you can eat well. Simply eat smarter.

4. Grocery Store Tricks and Tips

This chapter deals with the grocery store itself. I will show you the tricks grocery stores use to get you to buy products, how to not get tricked, and other things you can do to save money. The markup on groceries is very small so the grocers will do everything in their power to get you to buy the higher profit items from them.

Do not Buy Items from your Grocery Store that you can Buy Elsewhere.

There are certain items you should never buy in a grocery store no matter what, because you can always get them cheaper at a Target or a Wal-Mart. A good rule of thumb is never buy non-perishable items at a grocery store.

The reason for this is that because the markup is so low on groceries, the grocery stores will mark up these products many times more than other big box or dollar stores would. This is where they make the real money. The list is long and I am sure I will forget some things, but here is a little snippet of things you should never buy at a grocery store.

Never buy things to cook your food. Never buy utensils like pizza cutters or spatulas. Never buy pots or pans (including the disposable aluminum pans—these can always be bought at the dollar store). Never buy aluminum foil or plastic wrap.

Never buy toilet paper, paper towel, Kleenex, or wash cloths at your grocery store. Never buy pet food or pet supplies. Never buy hardware or automotive items.

Never buy anything you can get from your Walgreen's or CVS, like aspirin or ointments. Any medicine you need will be cheaper elsewhere.

Never buy diapers or things for your baby (except jar food) from the grocery store. Never buy powders or lotions or ointments for you baby.

Never buy charcoal or things to use with the grill. Never purchase items that are found in the checkout lane like gum or mints. Never buy air freshener or house cleaning supplies.
You get the idea. The grocery store is for groceries because that is what they do best. They will give you the best prices on food that you will find most anywhere.

The Grocery Store Layout

Billions of dollars are spent to examine shopping habits of the average consumer. These studies show what makes people pick up a product to look at it, it shows what type of music should play on the sound system to get you in the mood to pay more. The grocery stores know that items that are eye level will sell better than things on the lower shelf.

Billions of dollars are spent by the manufacturers on marketing and packaging. They create commercials that will appeal to you or your kids. They know what their brand name evokes when you shop. They understand that they need to grab your attention and get you to pick up their package. Once you pick up the package you will most likely buy the product.

Billions of dollars are also spent on product placement. Companies will pay the grocery store money to get certain placement on the shelves. They will pay for end caps. They will pay to have their products show up first in the aisle. They know that where there products are placed is more important than any other factor in the grocery store.

The items that do not make much money like milk and eggs, are always in the back of the store so you have to walk through the aisles to get to them. Everyone needs milk and eggs so they do not want to put them at the front of the store where you will come in and walk out right away.

The scientists also know that in America we tend to move to our right so almost every store you enter, you will go in the door and turn to the right. Usually the items to the right are the fruits and vegetables and other perishable items.

The most expensive items are at eye level. The items here will be recognizable to you by their brand name. The stores know that brands sell and that people are more inclined to buy from Coke than from Pete's Colas. That is the power of advertising.

The great thing that has happened over the past few years are that stores are now developing their own brands to compete with the national brand items. That means you can buy the store brand peanut butter or corn and you can usually save significant amounts of money. The stores are so confident that their brands are as good as the national brands, that they almost always offer a 100% money back guarantee on these products. And you know what? They are right. The products they sell are tasty, fresh and cheaper than national brand products.

In the old days the off-brand products would come in a can with a yellow label and black lettering. It looked like the yellow pages. The food back then was sub-par and as a result store brand food items got a well-deserved bad reputation. Since then grocery store chains have invested millions of dollars to develop their brand of different food items. They have invested in the packaging of these items to make them more appealing, and they have invested in the taste of the product. For instance, the peanut butter produced for the stores is most likely produced for them by the name brand manufacturers. They come off the same assembly line, albeit with sometimes slightly different ingredients. They taste the same, look the same and the only difference you will notice is the price.

This means that you can save significant money on items you use every day and the stores make more money on these items. It is worth it for the store to develop these products.

Costco had their Kirkland products. I have found that these products are often superior to the national name brand products. They taste better and they are significantly cheaper. Sam's Club has their Artisan Fresh products (formerly Member's Mark products) that compete well with the national brands. Wal-Mart has several store brands including Sam's Choice, Great Value, Equate etc. Target has their Archer Farms brands.

Other grocery stores have their own brand names. You will see these products next to the national branded merchandise and they usually have a sign pointing out how much money you will save by buying their products.

Besides grocery store brands there are "lesser" brands that are not as well-known as the products advertised nationally. In the cereal aisle, if you look at the bottom shelf, you will find cereal that looks like it might be generic. These cereals resemble the national brands except for the packaging. These items are usually in plain plastic bags and are nothing great to look at, packaging-wise. They are made by a national manufacturer, but they do not advertise and they do not spend money on packaging. The taste is close to that of the national brands.

Finally, the cheaper priced items will always be on the bottom shelf or top shelf in every aisle. These items are national items but they do not put as much money in advertising. The products are made with the same care and dedication as the national products but they are cheaper. Try a brand or two that you have never heard of, especially when it is cheaper. You will be surprised at how much money you will save by taking these small steps.

In my neck of the woods there is a store chain called Aldi. They are a cut-rate grocery store that offers a wide variety of fresh fruit, vegetables and meat as well as off-brand products for other items you will need in your kitchen. These items sometimes vary from trip to trip because they seem to buy from the cheapest warehouse or manufacturers' closeouts. They guarantee their products so you have no worries about buying items there. You can buy food here with confidence and you will save at least 30% off of your regular grocery bill.

If you have a store like Aldi in your neck of the woods, give them a try. The food there is high-quality, tasty, and all items come with a money back guarantee.

How to shop: Different Grocery Stores, Different Prices

We tend to think of grocery stores as basically having the same prices on food items. If you look at the ads, the sale prices of items are usually within a couple of cents of each other, except for the deals designed to get you in the door. Most people go to their closest grocery store giving up savings for convenience. Yet I am willing to bet that most people that live in a decent sized city have two or three different grocery stores in a five mile radius.

Add to the equation Super Targets where they have a full grocery store inside of a Target store, and the Wal-Mart stores with full grocery selections and you really will see significant price differences. The only issues I have with stores like Wal-Mart and Super Targets is that they do not have the widest selections available on all products like a regular grocery store does.

The one thing you can do is to put together a comprehensive list of food items that you use week in and week out. Things I would put on this list are items like milk, butter, bread, meat, fruits, vegetables, cooking oils, flour, etc. These are items that are the base for a lot of other coking recipes and these are items that you will buy week in and week out no matter what happens.

Make a list of 20 or 30 basic food stuffs that you use every day and then go and compare these items from one grocery store to another. Look at the normal, everyday price on these items, not the sale price.

Bring your list to each store near your house and keep track of the prices on each of these 20 to 30 items on your list. Bring your iPhone or a calculator and add up the price of all these items. Most likely one store will be significantly cheaper than another on these basic items. If you save $10 on these items every week you immediately save $520 a year. It is a no-brainer.

I love Costco, and I always scream it to the world. Part of the reason I love it is because I feed a family of four and I save a lot of money on most all products I buy from them. I have noticed, though, that basic food items are significantly cheaper than I can get them at in my regular grocery store. Milk is $2.19 a gallon instead of $3.99 a gallon. Eggs are about $3.00 for two 18-pack cartons, instead of $2.00 for a dozen. Meat is always cheaper (although you have to buy it in significant quantities) and I feel it is better quality as well. My favorite comparison is Crystal Light lemonade. I do not drink coffee or sodas so this is my vice. At the grocery store a package of Crystal Light is about $5.25 for a half dozen packets that each makes two quarts. I buy a 16 pack of Crystal Light at Costco for the same price. If I had purchased the Crystal Light at my grocery store I would have spent $10 more for the same amount of Crystal Light packets. Thus, even though Costco has limited selection on grocery items, the items that I do buy save me a ton of money each year.

Here is what to do to save money on basic food items:

1. Make a list of 20 items you buy week in and week out.
2. Take your list to the three or four closest grocery stores and Wal-Mart or Target to compare the prices on these items. Bring an iPhone or calculator as well as your list and write down the prices of each of the items at all the stores. The more money you save each week will translate into significant savings over the course of a year.
3. Compare the regular every day price of each item, not the sale prices.
4. If you comparison shop Costco and Sam's Club be sure to note the size of the products you are buying. You must compare apples to apples, unit cost to unit cost, ounce compared to ounce, etc.

5. Once you start to really pay attention to prices you will notice great sale prices and you will notice when your own store or stores have a good sale on items. You can always buy more if you find a great buy and freeze or store the item until you need to use it.
6. One store, or maybe two, will stand out for the savings. It might be that half the items are cheaper at one store and the other half cheaper at the second store. It might be worth your while to shop at two different stores for these basic items.

Things to Keep in Mind:

There are a few things to keep in mind in general when playing the grocery game. The first thing is that there are many different options to choose from on where to shop. Do not get stuck in a rut and go to the same store next to home just because it is convenient.

Next, remember to make a list of items you need when grocery shopping. Do not stray from the list. It is important to realize that the grocery stores make a lot of money off of impulse buyers.

Finally, you should get used to the idea of pricing things per unit instead of by the product size you buy. This means that you should look at the price per ounce, the price per pound or the price per each of an item. Buying items in big bulk packaging does not necessarily mean you will save money on these items if you price it out per unit.

Next, when you do find a great sale or great prices on items you do use, be sure to buy those items and use your new storage systems you put in place. That means put the older cans that were in your pantry up to the front and the ones you just bought in the back; that means freezing any meats cheeses you buy after you package them correctly to prevent freezer burn. I use a Food Saver vacuum unit to remove the air from the products I freeze. When you put these items in a freezer bag, use a permanent marker to put the date on the package. Meat lasts for about a year when you freeze it. Rotate your stock in the freezers as well.

There is a store called Aldi that exists in the Midwest, and they tend to carry manufacturers overstock items as well as many off-brand products. These items are all high-quality but they sell for a lot less than in a "regular" grocery store. Aldi will NOT have the selection that other grocery stores have, but their prices cannot be beat. Keep your options open as to where you buy your food and you will save money.

Trader Joe's is a national grocery chain that sells gourmet food options at inexpensive prices. They have many products that they sell under the "Trader Joe" name and all of their products are top-quality without the high prices.

Local farmers markets have prices on fresh produce that can be cheaper (and fresher) than what you will find in the supermarkets. Be sure to visit your local farmer's markets, too.

Is Convenience Worth the Price?

Let's say you go into your local grocery store in the main entrance. What is the first thing you see? Most likely you will notice right up front, a deli-counter. These deli counters have a ton of different items that are already made and they look delicious. You will see everything from hot food to cold food and salads ready to be picked up, taken home and eaten. The food there is great and convenient, but you know what? The markup on these items is incredible. You are paying for the convenience.

A simple macaroni salad is usually $3.99 a pound. For the same price you can buy all the ingredients and make your own salad at home for much, much less. It cost pennies to make homemade soups. The price of a high-quality soup per can is around $2.50 these days and you only get a few ounces. You can make an entire pot of soup for about double that price and you would have enough soup to serve a few different meals.

Down in the regular food aisles there are a lot of other items that are the same way, pre-made but overpriced. Frozen French fries cost a fortune these days for even the smallest package. You can buy a bag of potatoes and make your own fries at home for pennies on the dollar. They will be fresher and tastier, and cheaper. Microwave popcorn prices are getting higher each time I go to the store. It literally costs you pennies to pop your own popcorn in a pan, compared to more than a $1.00 per bag in the grocery store. For the pennies you will get fresher tasting and a lot more popcorn. Buying chicken breasts already cut up for you costs a lot more money that buying a whole chicken and cutting out your own breasts. Cookies cost a lot per package, when for the same price you can make double the amount of fresh baked, home-made cookies.

Small convenient packages of anything almost always cost more than what you would pay for the same item in bulk. Also, if they have to cut something to package it, like sliced cheese, that will be a lot more expensive than buying a block of cheese and cutting your own slices. I buy big bags of cheese at Costco and I use the GripStic to keep a tight seal on the package and reduce spoiling. I also take half the bag and freeze it for future use. Sliced pepperoni cost more than buying a stick yourself and slicing it. Fruit is much cheaper at Costco or Sam's Club, or even at a store like Aldi. Believe it or not some of the cheapest prices I have seen on bananas is at my local gas station. They use this as a loss-leader to bring in customers.

Look around you and think outside your comfort zone to come up with ideas on how you can save money. Treat is like a challenge or a game and you will want to win, you will want to bring down your grocery bill. Soon these new habits will become second nature to you and you will find yourself instinctively choosing the cheapest items, you will know where the cheapest staples are located, you will know each and every aisle of your grocery store.

5. Other Grocery Store Tips

Pay attention to the way your grocery store advertises prices. If something is on sale for "10 for $10" you usually do not have to buy all 10 items in order to get the sale price. You can buy one or two items for $1.00 each. Always pay attention to the fine print on the sale tags and if you can buy less for the same sale price, by all means do so.

Likewise, if something is labeled "33% More Free!" on the bottle, is it a better deal than a sale price that is 33% off the normal price on the normal sized bottle? The answer is no, even though most people's initial reaction is that the bigger bottle is a better deal. Here is where you have to figure out the cost per unit to figure out which is the best deal.

As an easy example, let's say that a package of detergent says, "33% More Free!" If that bottle of detergent is now 133 ounces instead of 100 ounces (the 33 extra ounces are the free ones) and it cost $10.00 for that bottle of detergent, you will pay about 7.5 cents per ounce ($10.00/133 ounces). If the 100 ounce bottle was on sale for 33% off, then that same 100 ounce bottle of detergent would cost $6.67 a bottle, or about 6.7 cents an ounce.

I always pay attention to the price of the groceries while they are being rung up. Stores always change prices on items in the store, or items always go on sale. These items do not always make it into the computer. A lot of times the stores charge you more for something that is supposed to be on sale. It is a mistake, so simply bring it to the attention of the cashier when you are checking out. Most cashiers have the power to enter the correct price immediately. Finally, I always have problems telling the difference between yams and sweet potatoes. If yams are cheaper and they get rung up as sweet potatoes, then you are effectively paying a lot more money when you do not have to. Keep an eye on the register as the cashier as she is ringing up your products and immediately point out any errors that happen as they happen.

Look at the items on the bottom shelves. These items do not make a lot of money for the grocery stores and thus are pushed to the bottom shelves. The quality of the products is as good as or better than the national brands that cost more.

The weekends are worst days of the week to shop (this includes Fridays). The 1st, 15th and last days of the month are also bad days to shop. Why? Grocery stores know most people shop on weekends or shop right after they get paid. The sales might not be as good on these days and the prices may be higher on other regular items. The days before Holidays are also bad days to shop since once again everyone needs food and they all do their shopping on the same day. Mondays through Thursdays are the best days to shop and you will usually find more in store bargains on these days.

Saving Beyond the Grocery Store

This section is dedicated to other ways outside of the grocery store to save money. It is a bit beyond the scope of saving money at the grocery store but these tips will help you save money on your food bill. There are several easy and economical ways to save even more money when looking at your food supply. They range from easy to things that will require a little work. I am sure there are more things I have not even thought of, but the following are tips that I use in my daily life.

First, learn how to cook. There are many ways to get inexpensive cook books. When you learn the basics of cooking you will discover ways to save money that you never even thought of before. The main thing to remember is a home cooked meal will always be cheaper than a meal prepared for you at the grocery store or at a restaurant. When you get good at it, and it does not take long, you will learn how to use your own ideas to stretch leftover meat or chicken, ways to make food ahead of time in big batches. You will learn how to cook meals that taste and look better than anything you can get in a restaurant.

Next, there are ways to make substitutions. Buy a cheaper cut of meat for your roasts. When you learn how to cook you will find the most flavorful cuts of meat are usually the cheapest. Also, buy big bags of frozen vegetables when possible. Frozen vegetables taste better than canned and hold more of their nutritional values.

Another thing you can do is to grow your own garden. Seeds are cheap and it is easy to plant seed and grow your own vegetables. Cucumbers grow so fast that you will have problems eating them all if you plant too many seeds. Tomatoes keep producing fruit in the summer until you will become sick of tomatoes. If you combine a garden with canning your own food, the amount of money you will save will be enormous. For pennies you can get a lot of vegetables from your garden while putting in a little bit of work.

Learn how to can foods. I make canned salsa and tomato sauce. I either use tomatoes from my own garden or I go to the farmers market and buy the bulk items that are for sale. I have heard it is easy to can pickles. It is important that you follow correct canning guidelines and follow recipes exactly so that the food stays fresh until it is opened. Canning food will help it store on your shelf for up to a year on most items.

It is easy and fun to cut your grocery bill almost in half. If you look at it as a challenge or a puzzle you will save a lot of money, more money that you realize you are spending. It will take a little time and very little effort, but when you accomplish the steps listed in this book it will be like giving yourself a raise this year and every year in the future.

Good luck and happy shopping!